Both Sides of the Story

THE DEATH PENALTY

Both Sides of the Story

THE DEATH PENALTY

Nicola Barber

NEW YORK

This edition first published in 2013 by:

The Rosen Publishing Group, Inc.
29 East 21st Street, New York, NY 10010

First Edition

Editors: Nicola Barber and Joe Harris
U.S. Editor: Kathy Campbell
Picture researcher: Nicola Barber
Designer: Ian Winton

Picture credits:
Corbis: cover right (Sion Touhig/Sygma), cover left and 27 (Mark Jenkinson), title page and 25 (Greg Smith), 7 (Greg Smith), 11 (Lake County Museum), 13 (Michael Nicholson), 15, 33 (Guy Cali), 34 (Tim Pannell), 37 (Imaginechina). Getty Images: 39 (Johnny Eggitt/AFP). Shutterstock 9 (1000 Words), 17 (jorisvo), 19 (Tom Gowanlock), 21 (Frank Jr), 22 (Zbynek Burival), 28 (Mark R), 31 (Leah-Anne Thompson), 40 (Robert J. Daveant), 43 (ajfi).

Library of Congress Cataloging-in-Publication Data

Barber, Nicola.
The death penalty/Nicola Barber.
   p. cm.—(Both sides of the story)
Includes bibliographical references and index.
ISBN 978-1-4488-7185-8 (library binding)
1. Capital punishment. 2. Capital punishment—United States. I. Title.
K5104.B33 2013
364.660973—dc23

2012021963

Manufactured in China

SL002127US

CPSIA Compliance Information: Batch #W13YA: For further information, contact Rosen Publishing, New York, New York, at 1-800-237-9932.

Contents

A Suitable Punishment?

The death penalty is the execution, or punishment by killing, of a person who has been found guilty of a specific, and usually serious, crime. The death penalty can be imposed only by a nation state after a proper legal trial. Executions carried out by organizations that are not states, for example terrorist organizations, are considered to be murder. However, many people consider the death penalty itself to be a cruel and inhumane punishment that violates the most fundamental of human rights – the right to life.

Capital punishment

The death penalty is often referred to as "capital punishment." The word "capital" comes originally from the Latin word for "head" and refers to the fact that historically one of the most common methods of execution was beheading (cutting off the convicted person's head). Today, other methods of execution are more usual (see pages 10–11). The types of crime that attract the death penalty are known as capital crimes. The death penalty is most often imposed on someone who has been found guilty of murder, but around the world other capital crimes include rape, adultery, treason, drug-trafficking and some types of fraud.

Human rights

Opponents of capital punishment put forward many arguments against the death penalty, which will be explored throughout this book. But at the most fundamental level, they claim that capital punishment is a violation of the rights that belong equally to every person. Specifically, they quote Articles 3 and 5 of the Universal

Value of human life

"It is by exacting the highest penalty for the taking of human life that we affirm the highest value of human life."

Edward Koch, US politician, from his 1985 essay "Death and Justice: How Capital Punishment Affirms Life"

Declaration of Human Rights: "Everyone has the right to life, liberty and security of person" (Article 3) and "No one shall be subjected to torture or to cruel, inhuman or degrading treatment or punishment" (Article 5).

Supporters of the death penalty argue that death by execution is not torture. They say that it is precisely *because* of respect for human life that the death penalty is important – if someone has taken a life they should pay with their own life. They argue that some crimes are so terrible that capital punishment is the only appropriate response.

Timothy McVeigh (in orange) leaves court in 1995, after his arrest for a bomb attack in Oklahoma City, Oklahoma, that killed 168 people and injured hundreds more. Two years later he was convicted and sentenced to death. He was executed on June 11, 2001.

The view worldwide

Since the end of the Second World War in 1945, the general trend has been for countries to get rid of the death penalty. More than two-thirds of all the countries in the world have now abolished capital punishment either by law or in practice (see panel). These are called abolitionist countries. Countries where capital punishment is still legal and enforced are known as retentionist countries. The situation in the United States is complicated because the death penalty is enforced in 34 states and banned in 16 others. In 2012, the five US states with the highest number of executions (since 1976) were Texas (481), Virginia (109), Oklahoma (98), Florida (72) and Missouri (68).

Execution numbers

In 2011, 20 countries around the world carried out executions. The five countries that carried out the highest number of executions were China, Iran, Saudi Arabia, Iraq and the United States. However, it is difficult to know exactly how many people were executed, mainly because China does not publish any statistics about its executions. Some experts estimate that the numbers could be in the thousands each year. In Iran, the official number of people executed in 2011 was 360, but reports suggest that the actual figure is far higher. In the United States, 43 people were executed in 2011.

Abolitionist and retentionist countries

- 97 countries have abolished the death penalty for all crimes

- 8 countries have abolished the death penalty for all but exceptional crimes, such as crimes under military law

- 36 countries retain the death penalty for ordinary crimes such as murder, but have not executed anyone in the past 10 years; some have made an international commitment not to use the death penalty

Total abolitionist: 141

- 57 countries retain the death penalty for ordinary crimes

Total retentionist: 57

(Information from Amnesty International, 2012)

A mock hanging at an anti-government demonstration in Bangkok, Thailand. Thailand retains the death penalty for a range of crimes.

Campaigners successfully turned it into an international human rights issue, and many countries signed United Nations resolutions to limit or ban its use. But supporters of capital punishment strongly defended the right of individual countries to make their own laws, and to decide on the matter for themselves. This raises a fundamental question about the death penalty: do governments have the right to put their own citizens to death?

Human rights issue?

One reason for the increase in the number of abolitionist countries in the second half of the 20th century was a change in the way capital punishment was viewed.

How is it enforced?

Is there such a thing as a humane way of killing a person? Around the world a wide range of different methods are used to put convicted criminals to death including lethal injection, hanging, shooting, electrocution and beheading. In a few countries, such as Iran and Saudi Arabia, stoning to death is a legal method of execution, although it is rarely carried out. Human rights campaigners argue that stoning is inhumane and brutal, particularly since death is likely to be slow and extremely painful.

Humane method?

All methods of execution, however, can lead to suffering for the prisoner. Even supposedly humane methods such as lethal injection can be extremely painful if not carried out correctly. A particular problem with this method is the involvement of medical staff. Although a doctor or nurse would be best-qualified to inject the lethal drugs into the prisoner, it is difficult for medical staff to take part because their ethical duty is to save life, not end it. However, the result can be that injections are given by staff who lack the necessary training or experience, leading to botched executions and unnecessary suffering. In the United States, some doctors assist in executions on the grounds that they can help the prisoner die in a more humane way. But they risk condemnation from people who consider their actions a betrayal of medical ethics.

Electric chair

The electric chair was developed in the United States in the 1880s, mostly in the laboratories of the famous US inventor Thomas Edison. The first public execution by electric chair was in 1890. Despite being developed as a more humane alternative to hanging, death by electrocution was often a drawn-out and gruesome experience. During the 1980s, it was largely replaced in the United States by lethal injection, although a few states still reserve the option of execution by electric chair.

Violent punishment

Some people who support capital punishment do not think that prisoners should be allowed to die an easy death. They argue that the small amount of pain experienced, for example, by someone convicted of a violent murder does not begin to compensate for the pain that may have been inflicted on the victim, and the continuing suffering of the victim's family. But opponents of the death penalty argue that such a violent punishment is inappropriate in a modern society, and that it only encourages further violence. They point out that in the United States, the murder rate is higher in states where the death penalty is enforced than in states that do not have capital punishment (see pages 26–7).

A postcard from the United States, dated 1908, shows a man strapped to an electric chair, awaiting death.

The Death Penalty in History

The death penalty as a legal punishment appeared as far back as 1800 BCE, in the set of laws drawn up by Hammurabi, king of Babylon. In ancient Greece, an Athenian lawgiver named Draco set out a law code that punished all sorts of crimes, both serious and trivial, by death. Today, Draco's name has given us the term "draconian," used to describe any kind of law that is considered unreasonably harsh.

An "eye for an eye"

Many early law codes made use of the principle that punishment for a crime should match exactly the injury or damage inflicted on the victim. This principle was known as *lex talionis* ("the law of retaliation"), and it appeared in the Code of Hammurabi as "an eye for an eye; a tooth for a tooth; a life for a life." In fact, the purpose of *lex talionis* was to ensure that the punishment was in proportion to the crime, and that a victim (or relative of a victim) did not simply take revenge on the offender.

The death penalty formed part of the law codes of both ancient Greece and ancient Rome. In Rome, violent crimes, arson (setting fires), poisoning and theft were all capital offenses. Methods of execution were often extremely harsh and included stoning, being hurled from a cliff, drowning and crucifixion.

"Bloody Code"

In England, the number of capital crimes gradually increased from medieval times until, by the late 1700s, more than 200 crimes were punishable by death. This system of punishments later became known as the "Bloody Code." Capital offenses included petty crimes such

Lex talionis

"If anyone is committing a robbery and is caught, then he shall be put to death… If a man put out the eye of another man, his eye shall be put out… If he break another man's bone, his bone shall be broken."

From the Code of Hammurabi (translated by L. W. King)

London, England, 1784: a mass execution at the gallows in the Old Bailey. At that time executions were held in public and drew large crowds.

as cutting down a tree, or stealing small amounts of money. However, because the laws were so severe, juries and courts often chose not to convict many of the people accused of such crimes.

Arguments against

In 1764, an Italian politician named Cesare Beccaria published an essay called "On Crimes and Punishments." Beccaria argued that capital punishment was inhumane and ineffective, and he proposed the abolition of the death penalty. His essay was read widely across Europe, and marked an important turning-point in the history of the death penalty.

Pernicious and barbaric

"The punishment of death is pernicious [hurtful] to society, from the example of barbarity it affords... Is it not absurd, that the laws, which detest and punish homicide [murder], should, in order to prevent murder, publicly commit murder themselves?"

From "On Crimes and Punishments" Cesare Beccaria

The movement for abolition

The English settlers who landed in the Americas in the late 1500s and early 1600s took the practice of capital punishment with them. The first execution in the "New World" was of Captain George Kendall in 1608. He was accused of mutiny and spying. In 1612, the governor of the colony of Virginia introduced the death penalty for a wide range of offenses including killing chickens and stealing grapes. As the colonies developed, laws about the death penalty varied from one to another, just as they do across the different states of the United States today.

Early activists

Cesare Beccaria's essay (see page 13) had a widespread impact in Europe and America. Beccaria asked whether the death penalty was either necessary or useful, and he pointed out that centuries of executing criminals had not prevented others from committing crimes. In fact, he argued that because death was a "momentary spectacle" (it was over very quickly) compared to the more lengthy punishment of depriving a person of his or her liberty, death was less of a deterrent than prison.

Beccaria's arguments were a major influence on early reformers in the United States such as Dr. Benjamin Rush. In 1787, Rush founded the Philadelphia Society for Alleviating the Miseries of Public Prisons to improve the appalling conditions in prisons at that time. He also argued that, far from being a deterrent, the death penalty actually encouraged brutal and violent behavior. During the 19th century, the work of these early activists bore fruit as many states reduced the number

Notable dates

1834: Pennsylvania becomes the first US state to move executions indoors, away from public view

1846: Michigan is the first US state to abolish capital punishment for all crimes

1861: in the UK, the number of capital crimes is reduced to four: murder, treason, arson in royal dockyards and violent piracy

1863: Venezuela becomes the first country to abolish capital punishment for all crimes

1868: end of public executions in the UK

Nat Turner is caught by a white slave hunter after leading a slave uprising in 1831. He was executed for his part in the revolt.

of capital crimes, or abolished the death penalty altogether (see panel). In the UK, reform began in 1808 to reduce the number of offenses in the "Bloody Code."

Slave states

While some parts of the United States abolished capital punishment in the 19th century, most of the states retained it. Some states in the South even increased the number of capital offenses, particularly for crimes committed by black slaves. In these states, white slave-owners saw capital punishment as an important method of controlling black slaves. Executions of black people far exceeded those of whites. For example, after a slave rebellion led by Nat Turner in Virginia in 1831, Turner and 55 other black slaves were executed. But in the hysteria that followed, many more slaves who had nothing to do with the rebellion were either murdered, or falsely accused and executed.

Some Religious Views

Justice

"Whoever sheds the blood of man, by man shall his blood be shed."

Genesis 9:6 One of the passages from the Old Testament of the Bible often used to justify capital punishment

Throughout history, most of the major world religions have accepted capital punishment as necessary for maintaining order in society. Many people have justified their support of the death penalty through passages from sacred books such as the Bible or the Qur'an. In recent times, however, many religious leaders have campaigned against the death penalty as a "cruel and unnecessary" punishment.

"An eye for an eye makes the whole world blind." This observation, attributed to the Indian leader Mahatma Gandhi (1869–1948), is based on the Hindu principle of *ahimsa* – "the avoidance of violence." The Hindu religion has no official position on capital punishment, and arguments both for and against the death penalty can be found in Hindu teachings. India retains and occasionally makes use of the death penalty, although this is very rare.

Similarly, several countries where Buddhism is a major religion retain capital punishment, including Thailand. As in Hinduism, there is no official Buddhist policy on capital punishment, but Buddhists place great emphasis on non-violence and compassion for all life. One Buddhist teaching states that punishment with excessive cruelty harms not only the offender but also the person doing the punishing.

"Lawful slaying"?

In general, throughout its history the Christian Church has supported capital punishment as "lawful slaying." In the 15th and 16th centuries, thousands of people were put to death because of heresy – challenging the authority and beliefs of the established Church. During

. . . or mercy?

"He that is without sin among you, let him first cast a stone at her."

John 8:7 The words of Jesus in the New Testament when asked what to do with a woman found guilty of adultery

believe that these parts of the Bible have little relevance to modern life. They argue that as most of these crimes are no longer serious offenses, it is inconsistent to retain the death penalty for any of them – including murder.

the reign of Henry VIII in England (1509–47), for example, an estimated 72,000 people were executed, many for "religious crimes."

In the past many Christians turned to the teachings of the Bible to justify the use of capital punishment. Murder is specifically mentioned in the Old Testament of the Bible as a crime that is punishable by death. However, other capital offenses listed in the Bible include working on the Sabbath (holy day), swearing, worshipping idols (false gods) and adultery. Today, many Christians

The most famous execution in history – Jesus Christ, crucified on a wooden cross. This stained-glass window is in a church in Stockholm, Sweden.

"Thou shalt not kill"?

Today, there is no generally accepted view about capital punishment among Christians around the world, but many argue strongly against it. They believe the Christian commandment that overrules all others is "Thou shalt not kill." They say that Christian teaching is based on forgiveness and compassion, and that punishment by death has no place in the modern world. Many Christian leaders campaign against capital punishment. In the 1990s, Pope John Paul II, head of the Roman Catholic Church, condemned the death penalty as an "unworthy punishment." This view has since been reinforced by his successor, Pope Benedict XVI.

Some Christians, however, strongly disagree. They believe that the use of the death penalty for crimes such as murder confirms the seriousness of such offenses and the value of human life. They argue that those in positions of authority, for example in governments, have a God-given duty to punish appalling crimes in this manner.

Justice and law

"Take not life, which God has made sacred, except by way of justice and law." These words from the

Brutalizing

" …the use of the death penalty tends to brutalize the society that condones it."

From the Web site of the General Assembly Mission Council of the Presbyterian Church, USA

Qur'an form the basis of Muslim beliefs about capital punishment. Shariah (Islamic) law is based on the teachings of the Qur'an that accepts the death penalty as a suitable punishment for intentional murder and "crimes committed against the community." In cases of murder, it is usually left to the victim's family to decide whether to ask the authorities to enforce the death penalty, or to accept financial compensation (known as *diya*) for their loss. The second category, "crimes against the community," may include terrorism, piracy, apostasy (turning against your faith), rape, adultery and homosexuality.

While capital punishment forms part of the law in Islamic countries, the way it is enforced varies widely from place to place. Some countries, such as Saudi Arabia, have a very strict interpretation of Shariah law and execute many people every year. Most executions in Saudi Arabia are public beheadings. In 2011, there were 82 executions in Saudi Arabia, including that of a woman found guilty of sorcery (witchcraft). Other Muslim countries retain the death penalty in law but are abolitionist in practice (they do not enforce it). A small minority of Muslims speak out against capital punishment, arguing that its use is based on a misinterpretation of the teachings in the Qur'an.

Legitimate option

"God instituted capital punishment as a legitimate punitive [punishing] option for every state... Capital punishment remains a valid instrument in the state's administration of justice."

From the Web site of the Southern Baptist Convention, USA

The Qur'an is the central religious text of Islam. Muslims believe that it contains the words of Allah (God), as revealed to the Prophet Muhammad.

Retribution or Vengeance?

The issue of capital punishment provokes fierce debate. Is it retribution (a just form of punishment), or is it simply vengeance? Is it applied consistently? Does it deliver justice to the relatives of a victim? Does it deter other would-be criminals? Is it cost-effective? These are the questions under consideration in this chapter.

Supporters of the death penalty argue that a person found guilty of a crime such as murder deserves to be punished in proportion to the seriousness of their crime. They believe that capital punishment reinforces the moral code on which society is based. Opponents argue that the death penalty is not retribution but vengeance. Killing a convicted criminal does not bring the victim back to life – all it does is needlessly take another life.

Arbitrariness

One argument against capital punishment put forward by campaigners in the United States is that it is not applied consistently. Some of the variation is a result of every state having a slightly different legal system and set of laws. But many opponents of the death penalty point out that criminals who commit extremely serious offenses can receive quite different sentences depending on where they are tried, the color of their skin, and the race of their victim (issues of color and race are examined on pages 34–5). They say the law is arbitrary (determined by chance) and therefore unfair.

Cruel and unusual

"These death sentences are cruel and unusual in the same way that being struck by lightning is cruel and unusual. For, of all the people convicted of rapes and murders in 1967 and 1968 … the petitioners [offenders] are among a capriciously [unpredictably] selected random handful upon whom the sentence of death has in fact been imposed."

Furman v. Georgia, 1972 Supreme Court ruling

Furman v. Georgia

In 1972, a case between William Furman and the state of Georgia went to the US Supreme Court. Furman had been found guilty of murder during a robbery, and sentenced to death. However, the Supreme Court ruled that in Furman and several other cases the death penalty had been applied unevenly and arbitrarily. Capital punishment was suspended in the United States for four years following this judgment, as states rewrote their laws. And although the US Supreme Court accepted changes to state capital punishment laws in 1976, many people consider that arbitrariness still remains a major problem in applying the death penalty.

The US Supreme Court, in Washington D.C., is where some death penalty appeals are decided.

Adequate information and guidance

"The concerns expressed in Furman that the death penalty not be imposed arbitrarily ... can be met by a carefully drafted statute [law] that ensures that the sentencing authority is given adequate information and guidance..."

Gregg v. Georgia, 1976 Supreme Court ruling accepting changes to the state laws

21

Justice for the victim?

Does the death penalty deliver justice to a victim and to his or her family? Justice in proportion to the crime committed (an "eye for an eye," see page 12) is one of the main justifications used by death penalty supporters.

Speaking out against the death penalty

"We had no control over what happened to our daughter, but we can choose how we respond. For us, part of that response involves speaking out for violence prevention and against the death penalty."

Amanda and Nick Wilcox, whose daughter Laura was murdered in 2001 (from the Murder Victims' Families for Human Rights Web site)

A statue of the figure of Justice in Dublin, Ireland. She holds a set of scales to represent weighing up the relative strengths of the two sides of a case in court.

Suffering of victims

"The attention given to the execution of 1,000 murderers is repugnant [disgusting], especially when the loudest voices think the death of a convicted murderer is a tragedy. Yet the deaths and suffering of countless victims is only an easily-ignored statistic."

From the pro-death penalty Web site ProDeathPenalty.com

In the United States, relatives of the victim are usually permitted to view the execution, either in person or by closed-circuit television. Some people argue that the execution of an offender allows the victim's family to "move on" from the horror of the crime.

Victim impact statements

In the United States, some states allow victims to make "victim impact statements." These statements are given after the offender has been found guilty, but before sentence is passed. They allow relatives to give details about the victim, and about the effects his or her death

has had upon them. Supporters of capital punishment argue that such statements are an important way of making offenders understand the impact of their actions, and for the court to weigh up the correct penalty.

Opponents of capital punishment have many concerns about victim impact statements. They fear that the strong emotions often expressed in such statements are not necessarily helpful or appropriate when sentencing is being considered. In such circumstances, they argue, lawful retribution can overbalance into revenge. As a study from the state of New Jersey put it: "giving victims the indirect power of revenge undermines the principle of government by law."

Traumatizing and unhelpful?

Some organizations made up of victims' families actively campaign against the death penalty in the United States. They argue that the death penalty focuses the attention on the offender rather than the victim. They say that this point is underlined by the huge amounts of money spent on capital punishment, as opposed to services to support victims' relatives. They say that the whole process of capital punishment is traumatizing and unhelpful to victims' families.

Life in prison

Some people believe that the death penalty is not adequate retribution for the worst crimes. They argue that execution is too easy an option, and that a lifetime spent in prison is a far worse prospect for many offenders. Others may argue that a life sentence is actually a better outcome for victims' relatives because it starts immediately once the trial has finished, and it removes the offender from the spotlight. For some, a life sentence has even more positive advantages – it allows for the possibility of rehabilitation (restoring to a useful life) of the offender, and of forgiveness (see panel).

Death row

Some people consider that the time waiting on "death row" – the area of a prison that houses prisoners who have been sentenced to death – is punishment in itself. Prisoners can spend many years on death row while appeals against their sentences work their way through the courts. In the United States, the average time between sentence and execution is more than 10 years.

Conditions for prisoners on death row are often particularly harsh.

The Tariq Khamisa Foundation

On January 21, 1995 Tariq Khamisa, a student at San Diego State University, California, was attacked by a group of youths while out delivering pizzas. When he tried to escape, he was shot dead by one of the gang, a 14-year-old named Tony Hicks. With extraordinary insight, Khamisa's father, Azim, quickly realized that there were "victims at both ends of that gun…." Together with Hicks' grandfather, Azim set up a foundation dedicated to tackling youth violence. In 1996, Tony Hicks pleaded guilty and begged forgiveness for Tariq's murder. He was sentenced to 25 years in prison. Azim believes forgiveness is central to recovery from such a crime – both for the offender and the victim: "The criminal needs the victim's forgiveness to heal. And in one of human nature's strange twists, full healing for the victim may require him or her to grant that forgiveness…"

A guard stands outside the cells on death row at Ellis Unit in Huntsville, Texas.

In the United States, death row prisoners are usually kept in solitary confinement (alone) and excluded from the education or work programs that are offered to other prisoners. In Japan, prisoners are also confined to their cells, with almost no contact with the outside world. They are not told when they will be executed, so they endure the mental torture that every day could be their last. The authorities argue that such conditions are necessary to keep prisoners calm, and to prevent them from escaping. Opponents of the death penalty believe that the suffering endured by prisoners in such conditions means that they are effectively sentenced to a double punishment – years of waiting and anticipation, followed by the execution itself.

Does it stop crime?

Is there any evidence that the death penalty reduces or deters crime? Supporters of the death penalty argue strongly that executing offenders saves other people's lives. There is certainly the fact that once dead, an offender cannot commit another crime. Supporters of capital punishment point out that many people on death row have committed more than one murder. They voice their concern that such murderers are very likely to kill again should they escape. They also argue that there are many potential murderers in society who do not commit a crime because of their fear of execution.

Opponents of capital punishment reject these arguments. They argue that the possibility of being caught and punished is an adequate deterrent to crime. They point out that very few murders are carried out by rational people who weigh up the possible consequences of their actions. Many murderers are people who find it difficult to fit into society, and most violent crimes are carried out in moments of high emotion and without any previous consideration.

No deterrent effect

"The death penalty has no deterrent effect. Claims that each execution deters a certain number of murders have been thoroughly discredited... People commit murders largely in the heat of passion, under the influence of alcohol or drugs, or because they are mentally ill, giving little or no thought to the possible consequences of their acts."

From the Web site of the American Civil Liberties Union

Slippery statistics

Crime-rate statistics are used by capital punishment abolitionists *and* retentionists to support their arguments. In the United States, murder rates are consistently higher in states with the death penalty than those without. The murder rate in the southern states of the United States, which account for 80 percent of executions, was 5.6 per 100,000 in 2010, compared to 4.2 in the north (which has less than 1 percent of executions). Some supporters of the death penalty believe this is proof

Deterring murderers

"If we execute murderers and there is in fact no deterrent effect, we have killed a bunch of murderers. If we fail to execute murderers, and doing so would in fact have deterred other murders, we have allowed the killing of a bunch of innocent victims. I would much rather risk the former. This, to me, is not a tough call."

Professor John McAdams, Marquette University, Wisconsin, speaking about deterrence and the death penalty in 2009

that more people on death row should be executed, to make the deterrent effect stronger. But opponents argue that statistics consistently show that the death penalty does not work as a deterrent. In Canada, for example, the death penalty was abolished in 1976. Since then the murder rate has dropped from over 3 per 100,000 people to 1.62 in 2010.

A lethal injection chamber in Texas. Texas has the highest number of executions of any US state – 481 since 1976.

Is it cost-effective?

Supporters of the death penalty say that in many cases it is a far cheaper option than keeping a criminal in prison for the rest of his or her life. But is this true? In the United States, most prisoners convicted of capital offenses spend many years on death row while their appeals work their way through the courts. Is this really cost-effective?

California

The state of California gives a good example of the costs associated with the death penalty in the United States. Capital punishment has been part of the penal code of California since 1872. It was suspended in 1972 (see page 21) and after several

Death row for male prisoners in California is at San Quentin State Prison, shown here. All executions of male offenders in the state are also carried out here.

years of legal challenges and changes, reinstated in its present form in 1978. Between that date and 2000, the number of capital crimes went up from 12 to 39. At the same time, the number of inmates on death row also increased rapidly. In 2012, there were 732 people on California's death row – the largest death row population in the United States. Since 1978, only 13 people had been executed in California. The overall cost to the state of administering the death penalty between 1978 and 2012 has been estimated at over $4 billion. The costs came from keeping large numbers of inmates on death row, but also from the huge numbers of lawyers involved in dealing with capital cases and appeals.

Capital punishment in California

- between 1976 and 2012, the average time spent on death row was over 20 years – prisoners were more likely to die of old age than by lethal injection

- in 2010, California spent about $70 million housing inmates on death row

- between 1978 and 2012, there were around 1,940 capital trials

- on average, each capital trial cost $1 million more than a trial that didn't involve the death penalty

(Information from the Death Penalty Information Center)

Cost and justice

Supporters of the death penalty argue that costs could be reduced if offenders were allowed fewer appeals. In countries where defendants are tried quickly, and are not allowed to challenge their sentences, costs are inevitably lower. In such cases, the cost to the state of the death penalty is probably much lower than that of life imprisonment. But many people have serious doubts about the quality of the justice delivered in many of these countries (see page 32). Opponents argue that every stage of a capital case is more complicated, time-consuming and costly, mainly because of the need to ensure that innocent people are not wrongly executed for a crime they did not commit.

Who Is Executed?

Across the world, standards of justice vary widely. In some countries that retain capital punishment, confessions of guilt may be obtained by torture, and prisoners may be denied any chance to appeal against their death sentences. The United Nations has established a set of safeguards for all countries that have the death penalty, to try to ensure fair trials. Yet despite these attempts to protect their human rights, it is likely that many innocent and vulnerable people are condemned to execution every year.

Innocence

One of the most powerful arguments used by opponents of the death penalty is the danger of someone who is innocent of a crime being executed. There will always be some mistakes in criminal justice systems. Eyewitnesses may wrongly identify a suspect, for example, or vital evidence may be overlooked. Once an execution has taken place, there is nothing that can be done if the dead prisoner is then found to be wrongly accused and convicted. Capital punishment supporters

Innocence in Illinois

In 2000, Governor George Ryan of Illinois stopped all executions in the state after the thirteenth wrongly convicted prisoner was released from death row. Governor Ryan said: "Until I can be sure that everyone sentenced to death in Illinois is truly guilty, until I can be sure with moral certainty that no innocent man or woman is facing a lethal injection, no one will meet that fate." Amongst those found innocent of their crimes were Dennis Williams and Verneal Jimerson, who had been sentenced to death for a murder they did not commit. New DNA evidence cleared them of guilt. In 1999 they, and two other men who were also wrongly convicted, were awarded $36 million in compensation.

A police officer documents objects collected from a crime scene. DNA evidence collected from such objects can be vital in a criminal case.

counter this argument by saying that more innocent people would potentially be put at risk if there was no death penalty.

DNA evidence

Since 1973, more than 130 people have been released from death row across the United States because of wrongful convictions. In many cases, DNA evidence has been the key. DNA is the "chemical code" found in every living thing. A person's DNA is unique to that person, and can be used to identify him or her. Even the tiniest trace of hair, blood or saliva left at a crime scene can be used to obtain a DNA sample, which can then be compared to a sample taken from a suspect. This evidence has been vital in many cases of wrongful conviction. However, it can also be used to remove any possibility of innocence in other cases. Supporters of the death penalty point out that, in such cases, the death penalty can be enforced with absolute certainty of guilt.

A poor person's punishment?

It is claimed that people on low incomes are far more likely to be sentenced to death in the United States than wealthier people. The argument behind this claim concerns the quality of legal representation for a defendant in court. Most people accused of capital crimes cannot afford to hire their own lawyers. Instead, they must depend on public defenders – lawyers who work for the court system in the US states. These lawyers are often overworked and poorly paid, and many lack the expertise to deal with a death penalty case. If they fail to present the relevant evidence to the court, it can literally make the difference between life and death for their client.

Many supporters of the death penalty dismiss this argument. They say that not only are defendants in death penalty cases in the United States *guaranteed* representation by lawyers, in many cases they are also given higher than average resources. They point out that most of the offenders who have had their death sentences overturned still remain in prison, guilty of serious and violent crimes.

Well represented

"People who are well represented at trial do not get the death penalty… I have yet to see a death case among the dozens coming to the Supreme Court … in which the defendant was well represented at trial."

US Supreme Court Justice Ruth Bader Ginsburg, 2001

Fair trial?

In other retentionist countries, defendants may be denied legal representation altogether. Some countries, such as Pakistan, have special courts that sentence people to death after rushed hearings. In other cases, one of the most basic human rights – to be presumed innocent until proved guilty – is ignored. Instead, defendants are presumed to be guilty unless they can prove their innocence. This applies to people caught carrying quantities of drugs (drug-trafficking) in Malaysia and Singapore, where this offense carries a mandatory (obligatory) life sentence.

(Opposite) **Evidence is presented in a US court by a police officer.**

Procedural errors

"'Death sentences overturned in two of three appeals,' the headlines said last week. But ... 93 percent of the 'reversals' [people whose death sentences were reversed] were still found guilty. The rest were not 'innocent,' but escaped execution because of procedural errors by judges, prosecutors, police – and most often, their own lawyers."

Peter Bronson, The Enquirer, *2000*

Race and the death penalty

"We simply cannot say we live in a country that offers equal justice to all Americans when racial disparities [inequalities] plague the system by which our society imposes the ultimate punishment." This comment by US Senator Russ Feingold (in 2003) underlines one of the central arguments about

the death penalty in the United States – is it fairly applied across the population? Many supporters of capital punishment argue that the race of both victim and murderer has nothing to do with the sentence handed out. They say that justice is carried out simply on the grounds of the crime committed and the laws that apply in each state.

A lawyer addresses the jury in a US court. In the United States and the UK, juries are usually made up of 12 people.

Race reports

Opponents of the death penalty point out that since 1976 victims of murders have been whites and African-Americans in almost equal numbers, yet around 80 percent of defendants on death row have been executed for killing white victims. They also draw on evidence that links capital punishment and race. One 1990s report in Philadelphia found that African-Americans were nearly four times as likely than white defendants to get a death sentence for similar crimes. A more recent (2007) report by Yale University School of Law found that African-American defendants receive the death penalty at three times the rate of white defendants in cases where the victims are white.

Capital juries

To sit on a jury in a capital case, a juror must in theory be prepared to pass a sentence of death. This excludes anyone who is opposed to capital punishment. Opponents of the death penalty argue that this means capital juries are not representative of society in general because they tend to include fewer African-Americans, and fewer women. Recent cases in some states have found that African-Americans have been systematically excluded from juries in favor of whites. In 2011, a prisoner named Darryl Hunt was released after serving 19 years of a life sentence for murder. Hunt always protested his innocence and, after two trials, was completely cleared by DNA evidence. What would have happened if he had been sentenced to death? He said: "I was one vote away from the death penalty. I had 11 whites and one black on my jury. If you think that race did not play a factor in my case, then you're not living here in North Carolina."

Death penalty and race

- race of defendants executed since 1976 in the United States:

  White 56%
  African-American 35%
  Hispanic 7%
  Other 2%

- race of victim in death penalty cases since 1976 in the United States:

  White 77%
  African-American 15%
  Hispanic 5%
  Other 3%

(Information from Death Penalty Information Center)

Who should not be executed?

Many people believe that certain groups of people should not be subjected to the death penalty. These include the young and the elderly, and those suffering from mental illness (see pages 40–1). In some countries pregnant women and mothers of small children are excluded from capital punishment on the grounds that their children will be unfairly affected if their mother is executed.

Gender discrimination?

In five countries – Belarus, Guatemala, Mongolia, Russia and Tajikistan – women are excluded altogether from the death penalty. In the United States, there were 58 women on death row in December 2011 (1.8 percent of the total US death row figure). Since 1976, 12 women have been executed in the United States. According to some people, the small number of women's executions simply reflects the fact that the most common capital crimes – murder, for example – are more frequently committed by men. Other people argue that the low numbers of women on death row are a result of gender discrimination – that courts and juries are more unwilling to

sentence a woman to death. Many of these people believe that it is unfair to treat convicted criminals differently simply because of their gender.

Young people

The execution of juveniles (usually under the age of 18) is prohibited by a number of international treaties, and the majority of countries have signed one or more of these treaties. In general, executing young people is felt to be a bad idea because they tend to be less mature and therefore less responsible for their actions. Some people, however, believe that there should not be a minimum age for the death penalty, and that

Immaturity

"The overwhelming international consensus [agreement] that the death penalty should not apply to juvenile offenders stems from the recognition that young persons, because of their immaturity, may not fully comprehend the consequences of their actions..."

Mary Robinson, United Nations High Commissioner for Human Rights, 2002

Sufficiently mature

" … at least some 17-year-old murderers are sufficiently mature to deserve the death penalty in an appropriate case…"

Justice Sandra Day O'Connor, disagreeing with the US Senate's decision to ban the death penalty for juveniles in 2005

Wu Ying, a Chinese businesswoman, in court in 2009. At this trial she was sentenced to death for fraud, but in 2012, while still finding her guilty, China's Supreme Court overturned the death sentence.

juveniles should be held to account for their actions. The United States was one of the last retentionist countries to ban the death penalty for juveniles: in 2005, the US Supreme Court ruled that executing people under 18 was a "cruel and unusual punishment" and therefore illegal.

However, despite the international treaties, some juveniles continue to be sentenced to death. One problem is that some countries do not register births, so children in conflict with the law may be unable to prove their age. Some may not even know when they were born.

Case Studies

The death penalty touches individuals all over the world, including defendants, jurors and judges, and relatives of victims. The case studies in this chapter may help to understand more about the effects of the death penalty on the people concerned, and on society as a whole.

Ken Saro-Wiwa

In 1995, there was international outrage after the Nigerian author, television producer and activist Ken Saro-Wiwa was hanged by the military government in Nigeria. Saro-Wiwa was president of the Movement for the Survival of the Ogoni People (MOSOP), an organization set up to defend the environmental and human rights of the people who live in the Niger Delta. Since 1958, when oil was discovered in the delta, the Ogoni people have suffered from the destruction and pollution of their land. Saro-Wiwa was their spokesman.

In 1994, Saro-Wiwa was arrested along with eight other MOSOP members and charged with the murder of four Ogoni leaders. All nine were tried by a military tribunal in 1995. At the trial, the lawyers representing the "Ogoni nine" resigned in protest at the unfair treatment of the defendants. Many witnesses who gave evidence at the trial later admitted that they had been bribed. Yet only ten days after the trial, before an appeal could be heard, all nine men were hanged. However, if the authorities hoped the executions would kill off MOSOP and its campaigns, they were wrong. Many people, including Saro-Wiwa's son, Ken Wiwa, continue to fight for the rights of the Ogoni people.

It's wrong

"[The] death penalty is wrong. It is an instrument of vengeance, not justice... I think it belongs to the past."

Owens Wiwa, brother of Ken Saro-Wiwa, speaking in July 2008

Maria Saro-Wiwa, widow of Ken Saro-Wiwa, carries a cross bearing her husband's picture during a demonstration in London, in remembrance of the nine executed Ogoni leaders.

on the country's death row, the Nigerian government announced it would consider plans to resume executing people. The reason given: to ease overcrowding in the prisons. Human rights groups in Nigeria and elsewhere reacted strongly, arguing that instead of hurrying prisoners to execution, the authorities should concentrate on improving the criminal justice system. Campaigners feared that corruption was so bad in Nigeria that many prisoners on death row could be innocent.

Overcrowded prisons

Today, Nigeria's criminal justice system still stands accused of corruption, unfair trials, and a lack of resources to help people accused of crimes. Executions were apparently halted in 2006. Then, in 2010, with around 870 people

It's a deterrent

"…nobody would tell me the death penalty does not deter people who would otherwise have killed other people…"

Joe Daudu, president of the Nigerian Bar Association, on why the death penalty remains necessary in his country in 2012

39

Competency

In 1992, Scott Panetti murdered his parents-in-law and took his wife and daughter hostage before giving himself up to the police. When his case came to trial in

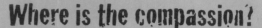

Where is the compassion?

"He did a terrible thing, but he was sick. Where is the compassion? Is this the best our society can do?"

Yvonne Panetti, mother of Scott Panetti, in 2003

1995, Panetti, at his own request, had no lawyers to represent him. The result was a conviction and a sentence of death.

A "circus"

The story behind these facts is that Panetti has a long history of mental illness, and had been in the hospital many times before he committed his crime. Before his trial could take place, it was necessary to test his competency – whether he was capable of understanding what he was accused of and able to cooperate with

An anti-death penalty demonstrator gets her message across.

Mentally ill, but competent

"Panetti was mentally ill when he committed his crime and continues to be mentally ill today. However, he has both a factual and rational understanding of his crime, his impending death, and the … connection between the two. Therefore, if any mentally ill person is competent to be executed for his crimes, this record establishes it is Scott Panetti."

Federal Judge Sam Sparks finds Scott Panetti competent to be executed in March 2008

his lawyers. After two hearings, the judge not only found him competent, he also allowed Panetti's request to represent himself.

Panetti's trial appalled many who were there. His bizarre behavior led one witness to ask: "How in the world can our legal system allow an insane man to defend himself?

How can this be just?" Panetti's sister referred to the proceedings as a "farce" and a "circus." In 1999, Panetti's former wife – and daughter of the victims – made a plea for his life saying: "I know now that Scott is mentally ill and should not be put to death." In 2012, Panetti remains on death row.

Mental illness

Executing people suffering from mental illness is prohibited by international law and by almost every retentionist country in the world. In the United States, the rule that prevents an insane person being executed was established by the Supreme Court in 1986. But the interpretation of who is sane and who is insane is left to each state to decide. The charity Mental Health America estimates that between 5 and 10 percent of all death row inmates suffer from a severe mental illness. This raises the question of what happens when a prisoner becomes mentally ill on death row, after being sentenced. In some states, such prisoners are treated to try to make them "competent" for execution, although such treatment is strongly opposed by Mental Health America.

Abolition or Not?

Every year, October 10 is World Day Against the Death Penalty. Despite a global trend toward the abolition of capital punishment, there are a few countries that continue to use the death penalty regularly.

Around the world

In 2011, Illinois became the sixteenth state to abolish capital punishment in the United States. It was the third state to remove capital punishment from its laws in four years, following on from New Jersey (2007) and New Mexico (2009). On the other side of the world, China claimed to have reduced the number of executions it was carrying out, but because of the lack of statistics it is very difficult to assess this information. The Chinese government reduced the number of capital crimes in 2011, but many non-violent crimes, such as corruption and drug-trafficking, still remain punishable by death.

Abolish now

"The evidence presented to me by former prosecutors and judges with decades of experience in the criminal justice system has convinced me that it is impossible to devise a system that is consistent, that is free of discrimination on the basis of race, geography or economic circumstance, and that always gets it right."

Governor Pat Quinn, March 2011, speaking about the abolition of the death penalty in Illinois

Several countries continued to make use of mandatory death sentences in 2011, including India, Pakistan, Iran, Malaysia and Singapore. This means that if a defendant is found guilty of an offense that carries a mandatory death sentence, a court has no choice about imposing the death penalty. Many people argue that such sentences violate the defendant's human rights because it is impossible to take their personal circumstances into account – is the defendant a pregnant woman? Is he or she mentally ill?

Toward abolition?

The United Nations believes that the "abolition of the death penalty contributes to enhancement of human dignity and progressive development of human rights." Organizations such as the UN and the International Commission Against the Death Penalty are working with countries around the world to abolish the death penalty. But many people continue to believe it is a curb on crime, and that governments have a legal right to put people to death to maintain law and order in society. There is still some way to go before the death penalty disappears for good.

The first World Day Against the Death Penalty took place on October 10, 2003.

Step by step

"Abolishing the death penalty is a goal for China's legal future, but realistically I don't expect it to happen in my lifetime…"

Qian Lieyang, lawyer in Beijing, China, 2011

"To reduce the death penalty step by step is a good method for China."

Professor Liu Mingxiang, Renmin University of China, 2011

WORLD DAY AGAINST DEATH PENALTY

OCTOBER 10

Glossary

abolitionist someone who believes in or campaigns for the abolition of something, for example capital punishment, or slavery

activist a campaigner

adultery sexual relations between a married person and someone who is not that person's spouse (husband or wife)

apostasy turning against or abandonment of faith

arbitrary determined by chance rather than by reason or principle

arson deliberately starting a fire

capital punishment punishment by execution of a person who has been found guilty of a crime in a court of law

competency in law, a test to ensure that defendants are both capable of understanding what they are accused of and able to cooperate with their lawyers

convicted found guilty

corruption dishonest behavior, such as bribery or blackmail

crucifixion a form of execution in which the prisoner is nailed onto two pieces of wood arranged in a cross-shape and left to die

death row the area of a prison that houses prisoners who have been sentenced to death

defendant in a trial, the person defending himself or herself against a charge

deterrent something that prevents or discourages an action

drug-trafficking the sale and distribution of illegal drugs

electrocution death caused by electric shock

fraud depriving someone of money or goods by cheating him or her

hearing in law, a type of trial

heresy a challenge to the authority of accepted beliefs

human rights the basic rights and freedoms to which all humans are entitled

humane characterized by kindness and mercy

inhumane characterized by cruelty and brutality

jury in a trial, the people who must give a guilty or non-guilty verdict on the basis of the evidence presented in court

juvenile a young person

mandatory compulsory; something you have to do

military tribunal a military court of law

mutiny rebellion against authority

prohibit to forbid

rape any act of sex that is forced upon a person against his or her will

rehabilitation restoring to a useful life

resolution in the United Nations, a formal statement of a decision

retentionist someone who wants to retain something, for example capital punishment

retribution a just form of punishment

treason betrayal of a country or government

United Nations an international organization founded in 1945 to maintain peace and security around the world and to promote human rights

vengeance harm or punishment inflicted in response to an injury or offense

violate to assault or harm

For More Information

Books

Opposing Viewpoints: The Death Penalty Diane Andrews Henningfield,
　　Greenhaven Press, 2006

Crime and Detection: Death Row and Capital Punishment Michael Kerrigan,
　　Mason Crest Publishers, 2005

Ethical Debates: The Death Penalty Kaye Stearman, Wayland, 2009

At Issue: The Ethics of Capital Punishment Christine Watkins, Greenhaven
　　Press, 2011

World Issues: Capital Punishment Alex Woolf, Chrysalis Children's
　　Books, 2004

Films

Dead Man Walking (15)
　　The true story of Sister Helen Prejean, who establishes a relationship with
　　a prisoner on death row

Let Him Have It (15)
　　How Derek Bentley was hanged for murder in the UK under controversial
　　circumstances

To Kill a Mockingbird (PG)
　　A lawyer defends a black man against an undeserved rape charge

12 Angry Men (U)
　　A jury in a murder trial decides the fate of the defendant

Web Sites

Due to the changing nature of Internet links, Rosen Publishing has
developed an online list of Web sites related to the subject of this
book. This site is updated regularly. Please use this link to access
the list:

http://www.rosenlinks.com/BSOS/Death

Index

Bold entries indicate pictures